FIFTY WAYS YOU CAN HELP SAVE THE PLANET

Also available in this series:

Fifty Ways You Can Help Save the Planet

TONY CAMPOLO & GORDON AESCHLIMAN

KINGSWAY PUBLICATIONS
EASTBOURNE

ISBN 0 85476 3651

Produced by Bookprint Creative Services
P.O. Box 827, BN23 6NX, England for
KINGSWAY PUBLICATIONS LTD
Lottbridge Drove, Eastbourne, E. Sussex BN23 6NT.
Printed in Great Britain by Clays Ltd, St Ives plc.

Contents

Introduction

For the Love of Creation...

Confusion, fuzzy thinking and unfriendly name-calling surround the Christian community's debate on our responsibility to the environment. This book is not a part of that debate.

Our goal, quite simply, has been to assemble fifty practical ways in which Christians can actually make a difference in saving the planet God has given to us. Our approach in the pages that follow is upbeat and optimistic. We want to encourage Christians whose relationship with Christ has led them to a sensitive concern for creation.

Having said that, we think it is important for those activists who use this handy manual to understand some of our motivations in publishing it.

Return to Eden?

Two extremes emerge in the debate regarding the environment. One group appears to be motivated by a vision to return this planet to the pristine conditions that existed prior to the Fall—a sort of utopian garden.

We are not motivated by this vision. All of Scripture and history point to the fact that we cannot return to Eden. Our entire human condition is cursed by the Fall, and that includes creation, which, according to the Bible, groans in anticipation of its day of redemption.

The other extreme position in the debate among Christians is that the world is essentially 'going to hell in a hand-basket'. Prophecy tells of the final destructive war, cataclysmic earthquakes and red moon, so why try to rescue something that is only going to get worse? If you can't fix it, why put Elastoplast on it?

Obviously, we are not motivated by this form of thinking either. We would simply point out a parallel.

Christians share the gospel message with many people, even though they know that probably only a few will respond. In the same way, Christians ought to be willing to care for the created world, even though they know that full restoration is not possible. We obey God because he is God, not because he promises us success.

Creation affirms God's authority

One reason we are motivated to care for the environment is that it is an awesome display of God's final authority over all of life. God created all there is. As the author of Colossians tells us:

> For by him all things were created: things in heaven and on earth, visible and invisible ... all things were created by him and for him. He is before all things, and in him all things hold together (Col. 1:16–17).

As we tend the garden we are acknowledging the rule of a higher authority over all of life. During our most severe trials and sufferings, when painful questions weigh upon our emotions and lead us to doubt the existence of an all-powerful God who is ready to come to our rescue, we can turn to creation for reassurance and courage. God did this for Job in his darkest hour. Job 38–41 is the Bible's best case for showing that creation points to the sovereign Lord. We quote just a few verses from the beginning (38:4–6):

8

Where were you when I laid the earth's foundation?
Tell me, if you understand.
Who marked off its dimensions?
   Surely you know!
Who stretched a measuring line across it?
On what were its footings set, or who laid its
   cornerstone?

Creation worships God

Scripture tells us that were we to silence our praises to God, all creation, including such inanimate objects as rocks, would burst forth in audible praise. Indeed, the silent praise of flowers in spring, blooming trees and schools of magnificent fluorescent fish tell the glories of an awesome Creator. And the near-overwhelming chorus of adulation from jungle creatures in the early hours of the morning renders our best choral attempts at praise insignificant. We go to the environment to listen to its worship of our heavenly Father, and we care to preserve it from destruction so that we can regularly return to be ministered to by its songs of adoration.

Creation leads people to God

The heavens display the wonders of God. Creation speaks of the One who holds all eternity in his hands.

Religious people have, since the beginning of time, been drawn to discover a personal God through his fingerprints on creation. This relentless search, which expresses the continual and ultimate aspirations of the human race, is in fact spurred on by the voice of nature, the masterpiece of God's handiwork. When we stand back to appreciate a painting or sculpture of a Renaissance artist, we are drawn to wonder at the superior gift. And these masterpieces pale in comparison to the ultimate work of art, the created world. We are motivated to preserve this display of God.

Our worship and witness

Every small deed of tending the garden is an act of worship. It is our bowed knee to the One who created the garden and calls us to live in it. We show by our care of the environment that we respect God's detailed work of living art.

And the converse is also true. When we mindlessly and perhaps arrogantly crush fellow creatures beneath our materialistic advances, we are demonstrating blatant disregard for our Creator. We are making an unequivocal statement that we do not regard highly the One who breathed and continues to breathe life into creation.

Another thing: our worship of God, displayed in our respect and care for the garden, is a witness to the people of the world. It is a witness because we are saying that we have found a personal relationship with the Creator. We have come to understand that the marvellous hand of God not only stretches a canopy of stars across the heavens each night but also reaches down to hold our hand. By our act of creation care, we are building a bridge to those who *do* glory in creation but are not sure that it points to a Supreme Being just within reach. They hope it does. If they could only find out how to join hands with the loving Creator!

This is our supreme joy and privilege. It is our opinion that Christians who stamp out creation in arrogant disregard are working *against* the task of evangelism, putting in place stumbling blocks for people whose respect of creation rejects a Christian answer to finding God because of apparent Christian disregard for creation.

And we would add: our destruction of the environment is a statement that we do not hold hope that God will remain patient in his return to allow more to come into salvation before that final hour of reckoning.

Ultimately, our care of creation is motivated by a deep love for Jesus. First, our taking care of the garden is an act of gratitude for the One who planted the trees and flowers and

placed the birds, animals and fish for our delight and suste-
nance in this life. Second, we are eternally grateful for the
freedom we have received in the forgiveness of our sins, the
gift of the Holy Spirit and the hope of living for ever in a new
world where there will be no destruction or decay.

We sincerely hope that this book will help you in your acts
of worship and love. We trust that these fifty practical ideas
will lead you deeper in your journey of faith and love. And
we are convinced that this concrete form of obedience and
witness to the Lord will help bring about both a harvest—of
people turning to God and growing in him—and a garden of
refreshment which will bring delight both to earth's people
and to the Creator.

Section 1

RECYCLE

Recycling is the simplest and perhaps the most important way we can care for the environment. The good news is that everyone can take part in this effort—and can really make a difference. The bad news ... there *is* no bad news.

We will suggest twenty ways you or your group can recycle. We recommend that you read through the entire section and then choose five or six ideas that you can realistically implement. Every bit makes a difference, so it doesn't make sense to overload and then give up.

There are several good reasons to recycle. The first reason is *waste*. Every time we throw away something, it has to be replaced. The cost of replacement is enormous. For example, a typical household in the UK throws away 3.6 kg of paper and board every week. At present, only about 28 per cent of the paper used in the UK is recycled. If we recycled more of our paper—and about 70 per cent of paper products could easily be recycled—we would save millions of trees in natural forests as far apart as Scandinavia, Indonesia and Canada, and help prevent the destruction of rare habitats.

It costs 70 per cent more *energy* to make 1 tonne of new paper than it costs to make 1 tonne of recycled paper. It costs about 7,000 gallons more *water* to make that same tonne of new paper than it would have cost to make a tonne of recycled paper. And a tonne of paper can be recycled up to seven times.

It costs to throw away (and therefore replace) metal. Every year, people in Britain discard enough steel in the form of cans to build ten ships. Americans throw away enough iron and steel to supply all the nation's car manufacturers—continuously. It takes four times as much energy to make steel from virgin ore as it does to make the same amount of steel from scrap. And as you might guess, it costs equally exorbitant amounts to replace other materials such as plastics and rubber.

A second good reason to recycle is *pollution*. When the dust-carts disappear down the road with our rubbish, the rubbish may be out of our sight, but it is not out of our system. There is no pollution-free method of disposal. Carting away household waste belches tonnes of exhaust into the air; rotting waste in landfills releases toxic gases; chemicals from waste seep into the underground water system and end up in our vegetables, fruits and taps.

A third good reason to recycle is *personal*. It is our lifestyle that creates all the waste and pollution, so in response it is our lifestyle that brings about correctives. Caring for the environment is a reflection of our worship of God the Creator. For this reason, each act of recycling is a form of spiritual worship. It is our personal relationship to God being expressed in tangible terms.

1

Paper Chase: At Home

The single greatest contributor to waste is paper. In fact, as much as 30 per cent of Britain's household waste is paper. Recycling paper is a relatively simple task and yet has enormous value for creation. The most seasoned environmentalists have incorporated recycling paper into their very lifestyle, and to them it is as natural a daily routine as brushing their teeth. This could easily be true for all of us. We've listed a few categories for implementation:

Newspapers

Most households get a newspaper, be it daily or at weekends. At present, less than 20 per cent of newspapers and magazines are recovered for recycling. Create a newspaper box in a convenient location that is dry, away from the wind and easy to get to (encourage the habit by making it easy for yourself and your household). Papers should be folded in half and, when the box is full, tied in bundles with string both ways. Don't allow yourself to read the next day's paper until the previous one is in the recycle box.

If your area doesn't yet have a kerb-side pickup of newspapers, then, when you are passing, deposit your papers in a paper bin—sometimes these are to be found next to bottle banks. Try not to make a special journey. Or consider supporting a youth club or some other organisation that sells newspapers for recycling. Look up the Boy Scouts or other worthwhile groups in the phone book to locate their dropoff points. Some groups organise skips for the collection of paper on certain days, say, once a month. Details are advertised in advance.

Almost all British newspapers now use some percentage of recycled paper. Because newsprint is easily recycled, you might be reading fresh news on old paper that has gone through seven editions!

Cardboard

Recycling plants love cardboard, as long as it is not glossy—glossy cardboard cannot be recycled as the coating contains plastic. Ordinary cardboard will go through several generations of recycling and will show up in any cardboard product that does not come into direct contact with food, as that would be unhygienic. You will be surprised to discover how much cardboard goes through your house. Keep a recycle box near the newspaper bin. If your local authority does not collect cardboard, and you cannot find a group which does, you can take it direct to a paper merchant.

Magazines

Magazines too can be recycled unless they have a very glossy coating (as much as 70 per cent of a magazine's weight can be due to the gloss), or have glued spines (generally, metal staples are not a problem). You will probably be able to dispose of your magazines along with your newspapers. Check to see if they should be kept separate. You may one day hold part of your weekend colour supplement in the form of packaging for your washing powder.

Other

Junk mail, message pads, study notes ... the list doesn't end. Keep a box for these miscellaneous items if you know of an outlet for them—some paper merchants accept lower-grade papers so it is worth checking and finding what guidelines there may be for sorting 'all the rest'. For sure you will need to remove the adhesive labels from junk mail and the plastic windows from envelopes before they make it into the recycle bin. Envelopes are not recyclable if they are the self-adhesive kind—these can easily be reused if you buy specially designed labels which cover the old address and reseal the envelope.

2

Paper Chase: At the Office

If you have discovered the volume of paper waste at your home, you will be amazed to find how much paper corporate Britain throws into the bin. The printer paper alone spewing out of British-used computers each year would stretch nearly ten times round the world. The American EarthWorks Group provides a graphic picture: Americans discard enough office paper each year to build a twelve-foot wall all the way from California to New York.

If you are employed outside the home, we recommend that you take leadership at your office to implement a recycling system similar to the one you put into operation at home. You'll need to use your creativity—for example, colour-coded boxes strategically located throughout the office for specific types of paper waste. A waste-paper basket next to each desk is an invitation for waste. One suggestion you could make is to provide fashionable recycle trays in place of waste-paper baskets and put the waste-paper baskets in a location where you have to move away from the desk in order to throw things away. Always make recycling easier than disposal.

Volunteer to empty the recycle bins and deliver the paper to a collecting organisation or paper merchant. If the merchant pays for paper, you may want to spend it on an office treat, or the office may decide to donate all its paper to a charitable organisation. You could *double* your recycling effort by donating all the money to an environmental organisation. Office waste paper is high grade and should fetch a good price. Computer paper, for instance, is about six times more valuable than newsprint.

One suggestion for the office concerns the *type* of paper your company purchases. Coloured paper always costs more to recycle than white paper—some paper merchants will not accept it. See if you can influence your purchasing department away from items such as yellow note pads, pink message slips and coloured copying paper. Be aware, too, that many types of recycled office paper products are now available.

3

Well Oiled

Used to be, every six months or so, dads across the country would crawl under their cars and drain the dirty oil. Discarding the sludge was no problem—it went straight down the drain.

Thankfully, we know better now, and few dads would want to be caught in the act (in fact, it is illegal to pour waste sump oil down the drain—the offence carries a fine of up to £2,000). We have learned that discarded oil makes its way into the rivers, lakes and oceans, destroying plants, fish and wildlife. Besides the damage to the environment, improperly discarded oil can hurt us: one quart of motor oil contaminates 250,000 gallons of drinking water. According to Friends of the Earth, around 100,000 tonnes a year of waste oil is unaccounted for in the UK, mostly from do-it-yourself oil changes. Corporately, we are guilty of much greater oil abuse than that caused by the fated Braer tanker.

Changing the oil in our cars is important to the environment. Engines run better and last longer on clean oil. So keep changing the oil; just be sure to recycle it. If you change your own oil, contact your local council to see whether your civic amenity site accepts used oil. Recycled oil, from which lead and other contaminants have been extracted, is used either as lubricating oil or for heating.

If your local council does not provide this service, a nearby petrol station is likely to accept used motor oil. Make a friendly contact first, to find out where to drop off the oil.

If you have your oil changed by a garage, be sure to inquire ahead of time whether it recycles. If not, find one that does. It's your oil, so don't leave the responsibility in someone else's hands.

One final suggestion: if you work at a garage, a power plant or some other business that regularly changes oil, find out what the company's recycling procedures are. If none are in place, volunteer your cheerful services.

4

The Plastic People

Some have labelled us a plastic society because of our use of 'plastic money'—the credit card. We are actually more plastic in our consumption than we realise. Here are a few statistics we've assembled from various magazines and books:

- Every year we use 2.6 million tonnes of plastics.
- Over a quarter of the plastics used in Britain goes into packaging. Almost none of it is recycled.
- Plastic waste makes up about 7 per cent by weight of household rubbish. Less than 1 per cent of this is recycled.
- Most plastics are made from oil—a non-renewable source.
- Eleven 2-litre PET (polyethylene terephthalate) bottles can make a man's pair of trousers or a fifty-foot washing line.
- Polypropylene, which is used for crates and battery cases, can be recycled and used for drainage pipes.

At present, very few plastics are recycled in Britain—less than 4 per cent of local authorities provide any plastics recycling facilities. A major difficulty is that over thirty types of plastic are used in packaging, and often bottles and containers are made from more than one type of plastic. This means that the plastic waste first needs to be sorted—it can only be recycled into high-grade products if the different types of plastic are kept separate.

There are schemes to recycle PET bottles—the bottles frequently used for soft drinks—and some PET banks exist. So far, however, only about 3 per cent of these bottles are recovered.

Most plastics could be recycled, but to make this feasible, manufacturers should clearly label the product to show what type of plastic it is made from (as they do in the USA), and use one type of plastic only in each container. Why not write to manufacturers to make this suggestion?

As with paper, take the lead at your office if you know where to take plastics for recycling. Certain industries, of course, use more plastics so you will be taking on a substantial task. Get one or more co-workers to team up with you. You can do simple things like putting a box next to the canteen door, clearly marked RECYCLE PLASTIC BOTTLES HERE—THANKS!

You may wonder where the material that is recycled ends up. Most of it is 'downgraded'—that is, reformed into a use that does not involve food. The sensible precaution here is to prevent contaminated plastic from ending up containing your next pint of milk. At a recycling plant, plastic is sorted according to type and then ground super-fine before being reused. It can show up in nonfood containers, carpets, ski jackets, rope and upholstery, to name a few destinations.

5

Go for the Metal

We use several types of metal each day. The most common form is cans. Each year, people in the UK use over 13 billion of them. About half of these are tin-plated steel and half aluminium. The USA recycles 60 per cent of the cans used, but the figure for the UK is only 2 per cent.

Recycling aluminium makes a great deal of sense. Every time an aluminium can is recycled it takes only 5 per cent of the energy, and causes only 5 per cent of the pollution it would have taken for a can to have been made from scratch. Aluminium can be recycled indefinitely, without damaging its structure.

Tin-plated steel cans are what our vegetables, fruits and pet foods come packed in. These are harder to recycle than aluminium cans because the tin and the steel have to be separated. However, because they are magnetic, they can be extracted from mixed waste. About twenty-five local authorities are now using magnetic extraction.

Schemes have been set up to increase the number of cans recycled. The Save-a-Can scheme, run by the Can Makers Association, provides skips which accept all kinds of cans, regardless of the metal content. Some local authorities and supermarkets also provide can-recycling facilities.

As aluminium is a very valuable metal, several charities collect aluminium cans and ring-pulls—as well as aluminium foil and milk bottle tops. Each can collected is worth roughly 1p. Find out how best to dispose of your cans.

Other metals that make it into our lives are brass, copper (your old piping and tanks), steel in other forms (your old car) and stainless steel (your old kitchen sink). All of them can be recycled.

Scrap metal is sorted for recycling at most civic amenity sites. If an item is too heavy for you to handle, your local council may collect it for you for a charge. Or you can contact your scrap metal merchant direct. Ask how he wants the different metals sorted, and then set up recycling bins at home accordingly.

And as we suggested for paper and plastic, take a look around your office. Be an environmental activist there: volunteer your services to gather, sort and haul away the goods. You will probably need some help, because offices sometimes discard recyclable metals in heavier forms such as old desks (remember the army-issue style?) and filing cabinets. For large items you may have to arrange collection.

As with other recycling, money can be obtained for these goods, and your home or office can end up with a little extra cash or can support a worthwhile environmental cause.

6

Get Some Glass!

If you have set up your system to process paper and cans, then you are well on your way to taking care of your glass. The most interesting fact about glass is that it never really 'dies'. You can keep recycling it over and over. It's conceivable that, properly recycled, your glass will outlast you!

Here are some more interesting glass facts:

- On average, each person in the UK uses 100 bottles and jars a year.
- Every tonne of waste glass saves the 1–2 tonnes of primary raw materials it would have required to make that tonne of glass from scratch.
- Recycling 1 tonne of glass saves the equivalent of 30 gallons of oil.

Before you throw away a wide-mouth mayonnaise jar, consider storing food (leftover chilli or salad) in it in the fridge. It takes less space than a flat container—and you can see what you've got.

If you're on the road and you buy a personal-size bottle of fruit juice when you stop for petrol, don't toss the empty bottle away at the next stop. Take it home and wash it out. Fill several with a favourite juice and keep them chilled in the fridge, for easy grabbing and low cost.

Certain glass items cannot be recycled with your regular glass containers. These include broken flat glass (for example, window panes), mirrors, coffee pots, lead crystal and baking dishes. If you need to get rid of such items, contact your local recycling officer for advice.

As for your regular glass items, rinse them out, remove the metal caps or lids and sort them according to colours— clear, brown and green (glass factories typically have to fill orders for specific colours). Then, when you are passing, take them to a bottle bank.

And again, we recommend that you carry the idea over into your workplace. Remember, every time you lug a heavy bag of jars and bottles to the bottle bank, you've saved a supply of precious resources. And you've reduced planet clutter by a bagful.

7

Catch the Contaminants

We probably are not aware of the numbers and amounts of toxins that sit in our houses and offices and pass through our hands during normal everyday routines. These have to be treated with special care, and kept separate from recyclable items. Here's a partial list:

- car batteries
- paint
- paint thinner
- glues
- charcoal lighter fluid
- nail polish
- nail polish remover
- oven and toilet cleaners
- garden pesticides
- antifreeze
- carpet cleaners
- wood and rust treatments.

Disposal of poisonous waste requires specialised help and advice. Don't dump anything which is hazardous. Instead, contact your council's Environmental Services Department.

The key elements are (1) use up everything you can, (2) find a safe place, away from children, where the rest can be stored prior to being taken away and (3) ensure a short storage life—that is, get hazardous waste disposed of as soon as possible. Some local authorities arrange 'amnesty' days when people are invited to bring toxins to one location; others provide a regular collection service by a 'toxic taxi'.

Paint and batteries can be recycled. You can recycle paint by combining leftover paints and using the new combination on a painting project that does not require a specific colour. Drop off your car battery at a local battery centre or garage, or a civic amenity site. Car batteries contain lead, which is a valuable metal.

Another obvious step is: don't buy more of these substances than you really need. When you can find a nontoxic alternative, use that instead.

8

Stamp Out Styrofoam

Recently, Burger King ran an advertising campaign in the States featuring a pyramid made from McDonald's styrofoam burger containers. That ad campaign was a brilliant, environmentally friendly nudge that influenced public opinion in the USA on McDonald's reluctance to switch to paper from styrofoam. As far as we know, styrofoam will *never* decompose—thus the effective 'ancient pyramid' image—and one little styrofoam cup or box will potentially damage a spot of the ozone layer the size of a football field! We're talking dangerous stuff.

Almost no one recycles styrofoam at this point. The process consists of repackaging it into plastic-type products, mixing the styrofoam with other recycled plastics. The jury is still out on the future of styrofoam. It is conceivable that a decade from now styrofoam will exist basically as an encyclopedia entry and in landfills from days gone by.

We suggest simply cutting out the use of styrofoam in your home and office life. Whatever styrofoam you do collect should be recycled if at all possible. Wash out those cups you couldn't avoid acquiring, and use them at your next few picnics till they start to leak, or to start off tomato plants or other seedlings. Use the tray from under the chicken pieces you bought—it can be a saucer under a potted plant or a snack tray for orange juice and biscuits.

9

Get a Charge

We would like to suggest a simple, achievable environmental coup: eliminate this country's use of nonrechargeable batteries. All batteries require mercury for construction.

So what's the big deal? Mercury is extremely toxic. It contaminates landfills and eventually makes its way into the atmosphere and water system. And manufacturing batteries takes fifty times more energy than they produce.

Take a look around the house to see how many batteries are needed to run your life. Here is a partial checklist for a typical home:

- torches
- clocks
- radios
- smoke alarms
- remote controls (TV, video, stereo)
- electronic games, baby dolls and toy animals
- doorbells
- Dad's shaver.

You might wonder whether battery companies own the toy industries: look around a toy department at Christmas and see just how many of the toys on sale require batteries.

Our suggestion is simple. Go out and buy a battery charger that accommodates a wide variety of batteries. You will probably pay upwards of £10 for a good one—less than next Christmas's battery bill. Put the charger in a convenient spot, ready for use, and then make an inventory of your battery-operated items. The next time those batteries fail, go and buy rechargeable batteries. Decide never to buy standard, disposable batteries again.

The next generation of children could laugh about disposable batteries in the same way that we laugh about the disposable clothes made in the mid-sixties. It can be done.

10

Hand-Me-Downs

At some point in our youth most of us feared being struck by the hand-me-down plague. Mum or Dad would pass on to us an older sibling's or relative's clothes. Being stuck with unfashionable clothes was probably what we hated most about this turn of events. Too bad Cousin Fred didn't out-grow that suit while it was still in style!

We probably are not aware of the number of things we discard that could be of good use to someone else. We may replace items not because they are worn out but because we have grown tired of them or have been given a new one as a gift.

Rather than throwing away such items, give them to an organisation that can ensure another life for them. Here is a sample list:

- clothes/shoes
- radios/clocks
- chairs/desks/beds/cabinets/tables
- garden tools
- television sets/lamps/vacuum cleaners/torches
- toys/games/baby equipment
- rugs/carpeting (including remnants)
- kitchen appliances (food mixer, kettle, toaster, cooker, can opener, refrigerator, hot plate)
- dishes/pots and pans/cutlery/cooking utensils.

We do not advocate giving junk to other people. That is

always demeaning and inappropriate. We do suggest that anything of value and use should not be discarded but recycled.

Go through your house, tool shed and garage. Make a list of all reusable items, and then contact a second-hand shop or charity shop. Alternatively, get in touch with a local housing association or your council, who may be able to use your surplus goods for families in need. You'll be amazed to discover how much you've abandoned that is in perfectly good shape. Many of us don't want to throw away items that we have replaced, so they just gather dust rather than finding a new home.

One practical rule of thumb in recycling these sorts of materials is, 'For every entry there is an exit.' If you get a new sweater or pair of shoes, you must let go of an old one. Ditto for clocks, chairs, toys and all the rest. This is not always practical—for example, when you are setting up your household for the first time—but as a habit it will prevent the unnecessary stockpiling and waste of items that are useful to others.

11

'Grey' the Garden

A large proportion of the water an average family uses each day could be used again right at home, assuming the family has a garden.

We have a suggestion that is practical only for those who want to take a large step towards recycling. It costs some extra time and money but can make a wonderful difference in recycling the precious resource of water.

You can replumb your home to redirect all of your water, except what is used in the toilet, for use in the garden when needed. If you have the cash reserves, and your water is metered, the cost of doing this will be recouped from your water bill over a period of a few years. A more straightforward method is to simply adapt a drainpipe so that water can be diverted into a storage tank or water butt. Once you have replumbed your home, begin to use soaps and detergents that are friendly to lawns and gardens. Most large stores carry these items. The water that you have saved is called 'grey water'.

Conserving water in rainy Britain may sound like a crazy idea. But a number of dry winters have led to the lowering of the water table, and many areas have been seriously affected.

The water piped to our homes has been treated to make it safe for drinking. Using water that has been saved—'grey water'—means less water has to be expensively treated with chemicals, and helps prevent sewage works being over-loaded.

12

Precycle

How about approaching the recycle campaign at the 'front end' of the problem? More than a third of British household waste is from packaging. We could cut back the amount of recycling we do at home and reduce the amount of natural resources used up in recycling (energy at the recycling plant) if we shopped with 'precycling' in mind.

Here are a few suggestions:

- Don't buy individual cans of drink. Buy the large containers and use glasses at home.
- Buy fresh, unwrapped fruit and vegetables.
- Buy long-life items in bulk when possible—for example, flour, sugar, rice, beans. Store them in containers at home.
- Be careful when buying savoury snacks. Too often these are divided unnecessarily into small packets. Buy the big packet and make your own personal-size ones if needed, using reusable bags.
- Be conscious of the number of bags you acquire at the shops—stationer's, bookshop, record shop, chemist, clothes shop, jeweller's. One or two bags would probably handle all these items. Just add new purchases to the bag you were given at the previous stop. Or carry a canvas or nylon tote bag.
- Avoid items that won't easily recycle—for example, styrofoam egg cartons.

Here are some interesting statistics that can motivate us to precycling:

- Packaging accounts for roughly 5 per cent of all consumer spending in the UK—£5,000 million a year.
- The average family buys more than 25.5 kg of food each week, of which 8 kg is packaging.
- A burger bag has an actual use-life of less than 30 seconds.

13

Reduced Use Zone Ahead

Your precycling habits can extend beyond shopping. Consider turning your home into a Reduced Rubbish Zone. When less waste goes out the door, fewer trees and other resources get spent in replacing it. Try some of these ideas:

- Save paper you get from committee meetings, school or the office which is printed on one side only. Use the other side for notes or writing rough drafts for school.

- Do the same with computer printouts. The age of computers allows us to print out roughs for correcting. Financial statements and proposals add tonnes to our cities' landfills every year.

- Whenever practical, use both sides of your writing-paper, reporter's pad or file paper.

- Say good-bye to paper plates and cups in home use. For picnics, you can use old crockery or durable plastic.

- You might go a step further and eliminate paper napkins. No-iron cloth napkins are simple to care for and add a touch of elegance to your table. Make a distinctive napkin ring for each family member and extras for guests.

- Go easy on the kitchen paper and tissues. Most spills on work surfaces and tabletops can be cleaned with the dishcloth.

- If you're an avid coffee drinker, purchase a metal coffee filter that replaces the disposable paper filters.

Be sure to apply these ideas at the office as well. Overcome the sense that you're being too fussy or stingy. You're being visionary and caring. Large businesses are catching on to the value of reducing waste. You're on the winning team.

14

Adopt-a-Neighbourhood

Once you have learned the art of recycling in your home, we recommend that you spread the good news. Our guess is that most people don't recycle simply because they are not familiar with how easy the process is. Why not transform your road, block of flats or school into a recycle zone?

Setting up the process would take a couple of solid weekends, after which maintaining the process could take as little as an hour a week. Begin with a little research: how many of your neighbours currently practise recycling? What is your local authority's target? Are there typical recyclable items that are heavily used in your area?

Once you have all the information, take action. If you live in a block of flats, be sure to work with the caretaker or managing agent. You will need to establish a central dropoff point at your building or in your area. This will include containers for items such as newspapers, aluminium, tin/steel, glass, oil, cardboard and possibly plastics. You might even donate a small portion of your garden to the cause.

If a good number of people join in, you will require help in transporting the material for recycling. Perhaps you can get support from a neighbour.

When the system is in place, get the word out. We recommend both a community meeting where people are invited to hear about the idea and a door-to-door campaign where you explain the notion and distribute literature clarifying the dropoff system. The idea will gain momentum as neighbours watch others catch on.

You may well find that the money gained from the recycling more than covers the cost of running the programme. You may even consider a surprise Christmas bonus for the neighbours with any leftover funds at the end of the year.

Once you are happy with how the idea is working, inform the local paper of its success. Your recycling efforts may get multiplied as others hear about them and pick up the idea.

15

Adopt-an-Office

If you have managed to bring recycling into your company, how about a bigger and braver step? If not too large, adopt the entire office building. You will need a motivated team of assistants, but once the system is in place it will run pretty well with little maintenance.

Here is how we suggest you proceed: let your boss in on the idea. Tell him or her that you want to carry recycling to other local businesses, using yours as a model of how it can work. Once you have your boss's blessing, do the research. Find out how many other businesses there are in the building, list their services, find out their current recycling practices and jot down the items they most frequently discard.

From this list you will be able to determine what kind of recycling centre you will need to establish on location. Be sure to get all of that in place, including the transport system, before going to the other companies. It's best to ensure that there are no hitches in the process, because people do not need any discouragement.

Make up a simple package containing four sheets of paper. Page 1 should be a very short note on company letterhead, signed by your boss, expressing his or her support for the idea since it has worked so well for the company. Page 2 would be '10 Easy Ways to Recycle', preferably done on a desktop design program. Page 3 would explain the location for dropping off the to-be-recycled material, and page 4 would give the names and phone numbers of persons to contact if there are any questions or problems in the process.

Take this package and go business-to-business. Inquire who the best person is to implement the idea, secure an appointment and then sign up another environmentally conscious company!

From time to time, go back to these same persons to see how the system is working for them and to suggest some additional ways to increase recycling. Once the system is in place and operating well, we suggest that you report it to your local council as a model programme for the entire town or city.

16

Adopt-an-Eyesore

For some reason, junk collects. Perhaps it is one of those laws of the universe: *Any void will eventually be filled with available litter.* We suggest a vigorous defeat of that law.

The rubbish that collects in open places spoils the environment and may end up in streams, polluting our water source, harming vegetation and killing insects and fish. Or that same rubbish may be picked up by conscientious individuals and thrown into the bin, where it is ready to head off to the landfill or incinerator.

Why not think of an area that needs a spring clean? This could be the land surrounding your workplace, school grounds, a public park, an area of woodland, a riverside walk, a local pond or a country lane.

First contact your local authority or the owner of the land you have singled out for attention to get permission for the project to go ahead. Ask the council officer in charge of waste management for the sacks you will need for the different kinds of rubbish and, if the clean-up is to be on a large scale, a skip. If he cannot supply these, get his advice on how you should dispose of the rubbish.

When you have obtained the necessary permission and fixed a date, find your volunteers. You may go so far as to approach the local press and radio. Or you may decide just to enlist people you know and local groups.

Before the event get well organised. Survey the area you

plan to tackle and take note of the spots that need a particular onslaught. Prepare a list of equipment that will be needed—shovels, wheelbarrows, rakes, and so on—and make sure people are responsible for bringing these items along. You will also need to put someone in charge of first aid. Warn volunteers that they will need thick gloves, strong shoes and tough clothing.

On the day, divide volunteers into teams to collect the rubbish. Have separate sacks for objects which can be recycled. Once you have collected all the rubbish, take a photo for future PR purposes and then go to a pizza restaurant to celebrate.

After the initial clean-up, you may need to plan further events to keep your adopted area tidy. If you decide to contact your local newspaper, provide your PR photograph and explain in a brief report what you have done. You may find others will join your campaign as a result of the publicity.

17

Convert Your Church

Every Sunday, thousands of people drive to church. The recycling potential of this God-loving, creation-caring group of people is just mind-boggling! Each Sunday of the year has the potential of becoming an environmental act of worshipping God. Unfortunately, and all too often accurately, the church has been accused of being insensitive to the concerns of the green movement. Well, let's banish that notion.

Consider taking on the task of converting your church to recycling-consciousness. It's the perfect setup: you have property, you have a newsletter, you have a transport system (members who drive there weekly) and you have a good reason—you all love God the Creator. Talk with your pastor. He or she may be willing to dedicate one entire Sunday to the issue, for starters. The pastor's role will be to preach a sermon on caring for the garden, and your role will be to explain how the system is going to work.

Again, you need to have the system in place ahead of time. Set up all the recycling bins at a convenient location on the church property (convenient in this case means easy access for a vehicle to haul the stuff away). Clearly label the different containers. Design a simple, attractive insert for the church newsletter describing how the system works. Members can bring newspapers, aluminium, tin, whatever you are able to pass along to a merchant or dealer.

Every Sunday, have a few teenagers serve in the 'green

brigade'. Their function is to collect bags from cars as they drive into the church carpark. This increases convenience to church members, gets teens involved, and creates more visibility for the practice (enhancing the likelihood that people will stick with the idea).

Now the fun part. The most underfunded programme in many churches is missionary outreach. Our suggestion is that *all* the proceeds from recycling go to a special mission fund beyond the regular mission giving. This fund could be turned into a special Christmas cheque that goes to each of the church's missionaries for personal use (something they always need). What a satisfying way of celebrating the whole gospel of Jesus Christ—that is, caring for souls *and* caring for creation.

18

Clean Sweep

Over time, large unwanted items collect in our gardens, garages and sheds. Some of the rubbish may be toxic, but typically it is 'stuff' that we reckoned we'd eventually get to. The problem is that one day, in a burst of energy, we do get to those piles. And typically what happens is that we load it all in the back of a friend's van and cart it off to the dump. We feel much better for having cleaned up the eyesore, but in fact we have just contributed to an environmental problem by stuffing the landfill unnecessarily.

Our suggestion is to take advantage of the human desire for a clean sweep and *organise* a co-ordinated effort ahead of an impulse-driven blitz. This is what you can do: get a clipboard and take a walk around the neighbourhood. Tell the neighbours that you are arranging a 'clean-up day' when a van will be coming door-to-door to collect any large items that cannot be set out on refuse collection day. Find out what sorts of materials they want to get rid of—couches, cookers, tyres, branches, paint, whatever. Get a general idea of what size task you're taking on. Once you're pretty sure you have a grasp of what's ahead, find someone willing to act as the driver and hire a van.

When the system is in place, go back to your neighbours with a leaflet announcing the pickup day. Tell them what time to have their material ready at the kerbside, how it needs to be sorted, and the cost. (This will be quite low if the cost of hiring the van is met by several people.) Organise a crew of volunteer labourers and assign them to specific types of recyclable items. Put the hefty volunteers in charge of scrap iron, cookers, desks and the like, and assign the petite labourers to lighter items.

Part of your plan is to deliver each item to its most appropriate destination: furniture and usable household goods to a charity that will take them (see 'Hand-Me-Downs'), metal to a scrap metal merchant, and so on. Anything which cannot be recycled should be taken to the civic amenity site. Check with all of them in advance regarding what they'll accept.

If you are able to execute this operation fairly easily, your neighbourhood and council will welcome a repeat every six months. You may even find the whole town catching on.

19

Elderly Aid

How about combining your recycling efforts with assistance to the elderly?

First of all, find out where the elderly are. You may discover that in your town many of them live in sheltered housing. If so, offer your time and organisational skills to the housing development in the same way you would for your office building or block of flats. First, you will need to contact the resident manager. Very often those who are working for the elderly are exhausted from the demands that go with that kind of work and so they cannot easily picture themselves taking on an additional concern. Your willingness to take charge of recycling will be greatly appreciated by them.

You or your group may be aware of where many elderly people live who do not receive the care of a larger organisation. Perhaps you know several elderly people through your church or fellowship group. Decide how many you are willing to help and find the best way to approach these senior citizens. It's important that you do not go to them outside an established relationship, because, sadly, many of the elderly have been victims of unscrupulous salespersons and consequently they are not very open to strangers.

Make the task as simple as possible. Most elderly people (with some dramatic exceptions) are not likely to generate as much domestic waste as other people, so provide one sturdy plastic dustbin for *all* their recyclable goods and a list of what they can put in it. Call in twice a month to collect the goods (simply sort the material into your separate containers on location), and return the dustbin to them before moving on to the next home. Use gloves to protect yourself from germs and cuts during the sorting process.

A fringe benefit here will be your regular contact with some lonely people who will appreciate your brief visits and your cheerful words. And you'll be helping direct some 'rubbish' away from cluttering the planet and towards new usefulness.

20

Start Your Own Company

Okay, here's the project for the real visionaries who have the time and business skills. Perhaps you live in a town where there is inadequate recycling help. This is your chance to stand in the gap!

Begin with careful research. It may be possible for you to act as a merchant or dealer—a kind of glorified rag-and-bone-man—and work in conjunction with your local council. Many do deals with private contractors. You will need to contact the relevant associations (see the resource section at the end of this book) to find out all the laws, pitfalls and recommendations that go with a recycling business. Once you are sure you're getting to understand the basics, talk with others in the same line of business. Nothing beats advice that comes from a practitioner.

Your next step is to locate property. If you are to do contract work for your council, there is a good chance that they may be willing to get you started with donated facilities. For example, Exeter City Council loans equipment and premises to Paper Chain, which collects office paper in the city. When your building is lined up and you have a sense of how much volume you are going to process, contact the recycling companies you've located that want to buy your product. Have them provide the shipping container and replace it every time they collect a full container.

With your system in place, get the word out. You may

consider beginning with limited hours—say all day Saturday—and then add hours as business demands. Publicise your services in the local newspaper, and be sure to give very clear instructions regarding what types of items you can process. Publish your payment rates too.

Section 2

WATER

By far the single largest death-inducing factor in the world today is contaminated water. Perhaps as many as 30 million people die from it *per year* and, sadly, as many as two-thirds of them are children under the age of five. To be concerned about clean, safe water is an environmental commitment that is very distinctly pro-life.

> Water, water every where,
> And all the boards did shrink.
> Water, water every where,
> Nor any drop to drink.
>
> Samuel Taylor Coleridge,
> *The Rime of the Ancient Mariner*

When the poet wrote of sailors adrift on the ocean, dying of thirst even though they were surrounded by water, little did he know how accurate a picture he was drawing of a modern society nearly two centuries later.

Water is contaminated through improper waste disposal, toxic waste, air pollution (brought down by the rain), runoff from pesticides and fertilisers, underground fuel storage tanks and sewage.

And water is scarce. Only 1 per cent of the world's total water supply is potable. Fresh water supply may one day be the world's chief weapon. The 1991 Gulf War demonstrated human vulnerability in regard to water when a major desalinisation plant supplying clean water to Saudi Arabia was threatened by an oil slick, and when thousands of

Kurdish refugees fleeing Iraq died each day due to a lack of water in their makeshift camps.

We suggest five simple ways you can make a difference to planet earth's future as far as water takes us there.

21

Check the Flow

We waste water every day without even trying and without even knowing it. Millions of gallons seep into the sewers without our help. So the point is, we've got to take action and check that flow.

Check your taps

It may appear to be just a trickle, but the little drops add up to an enormous loss of fresh water. Make it a Saturday project to inspect very tap in the house and outside. If you find any leaks, get into action. Let's hope that the solution is as simple as replacing a washer. If you know how to do these simple plumbing jobs, go for it. Otherwise, seek the help of a friend. If you rent a house or apartment, leaky taps may be the concern of the landlord. If so, contact him or her immediately.

Check your toilet

There are two ways in which your toilet may be a silent culprit. The first is a faulty valve that lets water flow into the bowl even when you are not flushing the toilet. To see if you have that problem, get a coloured water freshener for toilets (from your supermarket) and put it in the cistern. Leave your toilet undisturbed for ten minutes; then check to see if the water in the bowl has changed colour. If so, change the valve.

Another culpable deed your toilet may be performing is sending too much water through on every flush. You can typically cut that back by as much as a third and still get all the flushing you need. We recommend that you take a large glass jar, fill it with water, put the top back on and set it inside your tank away from the flushing mechanism. Voila! You've saved an equivalent amount of water per flush.

22

Reduce the Flow: Indoors

Nothing beats saving water like saving water. Our suggestion, then, is very simple: consciously cut back on the
amount of water you allow to flow through the tap every day.
Using figures provided by the Water Services Association we
have created a comparison chart to encourage you to conserve water.

	Saving Water	**Wasting Water**
Shower	Wet down, soap up, rinse off (4 gallons)	Ordinary (not power) shower (8 gallons)
Bath	May we suggest a shower?	Average bath (18 gallons)
Toilet	Install a jar or minimise flushing	Normal flush uses 2 gallons.
Washing hands	Full basin (1 gallon)	Running water (2 gallons)
Shaving	Full basin (1 gallon)	Tap running (up to 20 gallons)
Brushing teeth	Wet brush, rinse briefly (½ gallon)	Tap running (up to 10 gallons)
Leaks	Report or repair immediately	A small drip wastes 27 gallons per day

23

Reduce the Flow: Outdoors

We have suggested how to reduce water flow inside your home. Now let's go outside. We assume that you've already checked your outside tap for leakage. The issue now is to reduce the amount of water you use.

Caring for the garden

If you keep a lawn or grow vegetables or flowers, you need to water them. But you can take care to conserve water in the garden in three ways. The first idea we mentioned earlier: *'grey' water*. This is by far the most effective means to reduce water consumption, because it allows you to put back to work what was heading down the drain. Your second option is to carefully choose the *time of day* you water. Early morning and evening are best. If the sun is up and strong, you will lose a good amount of water to evaporation. Consequently, you will water longer to keep the garden green. Third, watch closely for any unnecessary *runoff*. Often a small stream of water ends up running off the soil on to a path. If you cannot operate the hose in certain areas without a runoff, we suggest that you water those spots by hand.

Cleaning the car

Our suggestion for conserving water while cleaning the car is this: *use a bucket* for as much of the process as possible, rather than a running hose. The impact is comparable to washing your hands in a basinful of water versus under a running flow.

24

Keep It Clean

At the beginning of this section we explained how polluted water kills. And the fact that only 1 per cent of the world's water is potable suggests that we ought to keep clean whatever little bit of water we have. We have two recommendations for keeping it clean.

Adopt-a-stream

Here is your chance to lead a group effort to make the country beautiful. Scout out the streams in your area and decide which one appears to be most polluted. Ask the National Rivers Authority responsible for your region if your group could have the responsibility to keep it clean.

Organise a workday to give the stream a thorough sweep, and as much as possible, sort through the retrieved rubbish for recyclable objects. Take advantage of the PR potential of this task and get a photo of your group in action in case your local newspaper considers your efforts newsworthy (you may influence others to get in on the act). Divide your volunteer group into subgroups so that every week someone is doing a fresh sweep of the stream.

If you would like to pursue this idea a little further, how about securing the help of biologists at a local school or college to find out about the natural vegetation and animal/

insect life that go with that stream? Learn how your clean-up efforts encourage the natural growth of God's handiwork.

Control the pollutants

Our second recommendation is that you take care not to pour any toxins down the drain. Also, reduce your purchases of these items, and that will diminish the chance of inadvertently polluting water with them, or needing to have them carted off to the landfill, where they're sure to make it back into the water system eventually.

25

Make a Career of It

Everyone can make a difference in keeping the flow of our precious water tight and in keeping it pure. Some may want to make a lifetime vocation out of it.

The opportunities in the field are endless. You could consider any of the following, for example:

- agricultural engineering (includes irrigation, water supply, drainage and soil erosion)
- civil engineering (work could involve the construction of dams, where environmentally sound)
- municipal engineering (among the responsibilities are water supply, sewage and refuse disposal)
- education
- public health.

If you are interested in discovering what the options are, and you are still at school, go and talk to your careers adviser. Or look in your local library for details of courses offered by different colleges and universities.

Section 3

ENERGY

Environmentalists predicted it for years, and finally it happened—the world entered a major war over energy.

The Gulf crisis will be with the world for many years to come. Fear that Saddam Hussein's invasion of Kuwait would lead to a shortage in the world oil supply resulted in a military response by the Allied Forces that has crippled the economies of both Kuwait and Iraq, created the earth's most disastrous environmental nightmare with the pollution of 700 ignited oil wells, left hundreds of thousands of civilians dead and caused 3 million civilians to become political refugees. We are more vulnerable to our energy needs than we know.

The world is unstable because of our dependence on energy resources (exemplified by the Gulf War). The world's energy reserves are threatened by our overindulgent lifestyle. And our use of energy from fossil fuels (such as oil) is constantly polluting the environment and hence, according to the Global Tomorrow Coalition, 'harming human health, causing acid rain damage to entire ecosystems, and increasing the buildup of atmospheric carbon dioxide and the likelihood of global warming and climate instability.'

We're concerned. Here are five simple steps many of us could take to conserve energy.

26

Go Natural

Well, almost.

There are ways to keep yourself warm without consuming too much energy.

Keeping warm

First of all, experiment with your thermostat. You may have more heat pouring through the system than is really necessary. A well-insulated house does not need to be heated above 20°C, 68°F. If your house is not well insulated, pushing the thermostat higher only warms the snow outside. You may find that you are comfortable with the thermostat set as low as 17°C, 63°F. Turning down the thermostat by 1°C, 2°F, will save you about 10 per cent of your heating bill.

If your home is empty during the day, make sure the thermostat is lowered. At night, don't warm all the house with the boiler; take advantage of heavy pyjamas, flannel sheets and lots of blankets or a good duvet to keep warm. Again, try this with the thermostat set low.

Think of certain areas of the house as your 'living quarters' during the winter's worst. Turn off the radiators and close the doors in the rest of the house, and keep your energy drain confined to that smaller area. This, too, will help to insulate your home further from the outside (closed-off rooms provide an air lock). Include the kitchen in your living quarters. The heat generated by your cooker and refrigerator will help keep the temperature up.

27

Patch the Leaks

Here is a depressing fact: the Centre for Alternative Technology has calculated that in the average British home 20 per cent of the heating goes through the roof, 25 per cent through the walls, 10 per cent through the windows, 10 per cent through the floor and 10 per cent in draughts—a total loss of 75 per cent.

We can do something about that. Here are some suggestions.

Check the insulation of your loft. In many houses this is no more than 50 mm thick. Ideally, it should be 150 mm. With an annual saving of £60 to £70 on your fuel bill, you will recover the cost in about two years if you have fitted the insulation yourself; three to five years if the work has been carried out by a contractor.

If your house has cavity walls, consider having them insulated with cavity filler. Mineral fibre is the best choice ecologically. This work must be done by a professional, but can pay for itself in four years.

Reduce heat loss through windows. Professionally-fitted double-glazing is effective but very expensive. Cheaper alternatives are secondary glazing which can be fitted by an enthusiastic DIYer, draught-proofing or heavy, lined curtains.

Try to stop those draughts that sneak under doors. The remedy can be as simple as a stuffed draught-excluder, even if it comes in the shape of a dachshund! The insulation of floors can be improved by sealing gaps and fitting a thick underlay to your carpets.

If you want to see how energy efficient your home really is, you should have a home energy audit. For this you may pay a fee, but as a result you should cut down on the amount of energy you use (and the bills you pay), thus reducing the amount of carbon dioxide being released into the atmosphere and ensuring that the world's energy supply lasts longer. Home energy audits can be obtained through some building societies, fuel utilities and trade associations. Also, British Gas and the regional electricity companies now operate special telephone lines offering free and impartial advice on the efficient use of gas or electricity, and gas and electrical appliances.

28

Step in Line

Every year the majority of cars in Britain produce four times their own weight in carbon dioxide. It may be customary to express our individualism and independence through our motor vehicles, but it is also lethal. More than that, it makes us *dependent* (contrary to our self-perception) in that we require the resources and co-operation of other nations. The Gulf War illustrates that all too clearly.

We propose a few very simple lifestyle changes that could make a big difference in the environment and the availability of resources.

Feet first

First, walk or ride a bike whenever possible. Every step you take with your own feet is a positive and important contribution to a better world. And it is probably good for your body too.

Go public

Second, may we suggest public transport? Towns and cities offer it, and once you begin to incorporate the system into your lifestyle you will wonder how you ever got along without it. Someone else fights the traffic, gets the heartburn and suffers frayed nerves. You read the paper or your favourite novel.

Go together

Third, we suggest that you car-pool whenever possible. If you work for a large firm and cannot use public transport, look for people ready to share the journey with you.

Finally, if you must drive alone, think through your errands and combine them so that you make as few solo trips as possible.

29

Go Light on Lights

If you are not sure of the benefits of keeping your lights low, take a reading from your electricity meter, leave them all on around the clock for a full week, and then take a second reading from the meter. The drain on energy resources and your chequebook will be significant.

Although this idea is quite uncomplicated, we consider it very important. We have two suggestions in particular.

Turn them off

Just don't use the lights when you don't have to. 'Any unoccupied room is an unlit room' is a simple enough guideline to follow. More than 20 per cent of Britain's electricity is used for lighting, and approximately half is wasted on lights being left on in empty rooms, or as heat produced by inefficient bulbs.

Change the bulbs

It takes a little extra cash, but you can buy energy-saving bulbs instead of ordinary filament light bulbs. The bulbs cost considerably more but use 75 per cent less energy than standard bulbs and last eight times as long. By the end of their lifetime they will have saved you £25 or more. Or you can change to fluorescent lights. Fluorescent lights are most efficient when left on (that's right) for a couple of hours, so choose the rooms in your house where you are most likely to spend two or more hours at a time each day. Consult your friendly electrician when you are ready to make the switch.

30

Watch Those Appliances

You may have some energy busters in your home. Some
appliances are just plain nasty to the environment. They
consume much more energy than they need to produce the
intended effect.

When your washing machine's day is done, your refrigerator packs up or your television self-destructs, replace it with
an energy-efficient model. Many modern appliances use far
less energy than older models—up to 70 per cent less
energy. Ask your retailer for the information you need. The
Energy Efficiency Office's green energy labels give an
appliance's energy efficiency rating and annual consumption.

Be sensible, too, about how you use your electrical
appliances. Take the washing machine, for example. Few
clothes nowadays need to be washed on a hot wash cycle;
40°C is adequate for most fabrics. This uses a quarter of the
energy of the hottest cycle. Position your refrigerator in a
cool place away from the cooker or a radiator, and keep your
freezer defrosted and full for efficient running.

Just beginning?

Perhaps you are setting up home for the first time and are in
a position to buy your major appliances. If so, this is a time
for 'precycling'. Look at the energy-usage information
labels. Find out from the Consumers' Association magazine

Which? which brands are reliable, and then pick the brand that both fits your budget and goes easy on the environment.

If you are in a position to put in a new heating system, be sure to get advice on what type of system will give you the comfort you need while being good to the air and easy on the energy supply. Consult your utility companies.

Try the sun

If you have spare money, consider taking advantage of the sun. Solar energy can heat up to half the amount of hot water you use each year. Solar collector panels are best positioned on a south-facing roof. The sun's radiation is used to heat a liquid, and that heat is transferred to the hot water tank. Solar water heating systems work even when there is no direct sunshine, though the brighter the day, the more heat is collected.

Section 4

SHOP GREEN

Our approach in this section on 'shopping green' is really quite straightforward. If we're going to recycle goods, then let's buy those goods once they show up in a recycled form, and in our buying let's demonstrate a clear commitment to companies and products that are friendly to God's planet.

Consumers have much more power than they realise. Companies will change entire policies if they fear that the consumer will abandon them. Your careful shopping is a positive vote for a healthy planet, and through it you join forces with a very large number of others who have begun to understand the force behind their chequebooks.

Every trip you make to the shops can be an act of environmental stewardship. We suggest five ways you can make a difference at the cash register.

31

Green Gifts

Is it true that most people in Britain have everything they really need? It seems that way at Christmas and on birthdays. Here is a great opportunity to buy green. Your gifts will probably be something your friends and relatives have never received before, and this kind of gift can educate them regarding our planet's need for friendly care. We suggest the following possibilities:

- Give a gift subscription to Greenpeace or Friends of the Earth.
- Get the gift catalogue from Greenpeace, Friends of the Earth Trading, Tearcraft or Traidcraft and order gift items.
- Look for games that teach about the environment.
- Purchase greeting cards that are clearly marked as recycled.
- Find an easy-to-read book (such as this one?) that will help the person take specific steps towards caring for the planet.
- Give a small tree or plant with gardening instructions.
- Give a pledge to buy tickets for an exhibition or activity that encourages love for nature—for example, a zoo or bird sanctuary.
- Offer a picnic lunch in conjunction with a nature walk on a day of their choosing.

- Give a coupon that is good for two or three hours of your services to help set up a recycling centre in their home.
- Finally, give a labour coupon that offers your services to spend half a day with them doing a clean sweep of their garden, garage and whatever else needs a little environmental attention.

32

Buy Local

The less distance your product has to travel to get to you, the less fuel burned, the less wear on tyres, the less packaging (and hence waste) needed, the less climate control required (and hence less energy consumed) and the less likelihood that certain preservatives (toxins) are added to your food (and thus the water system eventually) to keep it looking good till it gets to your kitchen.

Is that a case for buying local?

We think so.

Check out your store

Do a little research. Find out from your supermarket manager where the store's products hail from. Let him or her know that you are interested in buying locally as much as possible, and ask for a tour of the produce, meat, cheese, milk and fruit sections. Be as specific as possible. If you live in a small town, you have a much better chance of getting co-operation. Offer your creativity to a willing grocer. Suggest the creation of a special green label that sports the message 'Locally Grown'. Put an ad in the local paper announcing this innovation, and ask the editors for their co-operation in explaining to the public the environmental value of supporting regional producers. Local growers will be behind you for sure!

Encourage farm co-ops

If allotments nearby are available for growing vegetables and fruit, join with some others who understand the value of a unified effort to produce your own food. The idea of a co-op is that everyone puts in a proportional amount of money and labour to reap a proportional reward. If you are business-oriented, you might even experiment with this idea as something that could grow into a large regional company—then, of course, you would have to rent or buy land.

Green market

Some towns have weekly markets, which are always popular. If you or your co-op have plenty of excess produce, why not rent a stall and sell it to the public? People who are used to getting everything canned and highly processed enjoy handling food a little closer to its original state. If you have grown your fruit and vegetables organically, it will be in great demand. And the weekly sojourn becomes a time of socialising with new friends.

33

Look for the Labels

You may be surprised by the degree to which environmentally friendly products are making their way into the shops. It may require an extra few minutes every time you shop to check out the labels, but it is well worth your while if you want to work for a better environment.

Basically, you are interested in knowing whether the product was made from or packaged with exclusively virgin materials or whether the manufacturer took the care to recyle. You also need to know what effect the manufacture of a product has on the environment, what its effect is when used and what damage it might cause when disposed of.

Beware of labels which say something as vague as 'Environmentally Friendly'. Look for more detailed information.

The types of items you most want to check on are the following:

- Paper products. Are they made of recycled paper?
- Cleaning materials. The majority contain chemicals which eventually make their way into lakes and rivers where they harm plant and animal life. Some end up in our food and drinking water. Look for products which are non-toxic and biodegradable.
- Cosmetics and toiletries. When buying these make sure they are marked 'Cruelty-free' and 'Not Tested on Animals'.

- Fruit and vegetables. The fertilisers used in large quantities by most farmers end up in lakes and streams and eventually in our tap water. Chemical pesticides are poisons and pesticide residues contaminate food. So look out for food labelled 'Organically Grown', which has been produced without artificial fertilisers or pesticides. An increase in demand will lead to an increase in supply.
- Timber and products made from wood. Try to avoid tropical hardwoods. Alternatives are temperate beech or oak. If you must buy a tropical hardwood, make sure it is plantation-grown timber. Look for the Friends of the Earth Good Wood seal of approval.

We've already suggested that you 'precycle' at the shops, and that involves both buying products that are not over-packaged (leading to more waste) and buying materials that you know are easily recycled or made from recycled material.

34

Buying Big

It would be ridiculous to think about the environment when buying small everday items and not when purchasing something as important as a house. If you are about to become a home owner or are thinking of moving house you are entering an enormous realm of environmental consideration. Here are some of the typical environmental questions that go with owning a house:

- Is it insulated?
- Does the heating system reflect low energy usage? Will you have solar options?
- If recently constructed, has the timber come from a sustainable source?
- Are the windows climate-proof?
- Does the construction take advantage of the sun's patterns?

Be sure to check with utility companies to see whether there are any other questions or considerations that are worth exploring. For a while it was fashionable to buy homes mainly as an investment. Moves were made quite regularly. That pattern is shifting as citizens are reflecting on the value of a quieter, more stable lifestyle. So think long-term. Which means think environmentally sound.

The other 'big buy' you will probably consider is a vehicle. If possible, stay away from two types—diesel engines, because they spew unacceptable amounts of sulphur into the atmosphere, and vehicles which will not run on unleaded petrol (older used cars), because they put poisonous lead back into the atmosphere. Then look for vehicles that consume less fuel. And have a catalytic converter fitted if possible. Catalytic converters chemically convert at least 90 per cent of carbon monoxide, nitrogen oxides and hydrogen emissions into water, nitrogen and carbon dioxide.

Finally, if you are considering organising carpooling, sound out your company and friends and co-workers to see how likely that option is, and then investigate the possibility of purchasing a minibus. You will obviously sacrifice mileage on the vehicle, but you will more than make it up due to the fact that several other vehicles will be in their garages rather than on the road.

35

Boycott Buying

Our final suggestion in this 'Shop Green' section is that you specifically avoid certain products. We have already explained how toxins and nonbiodegradable products harm our environment, so we just list for you some products to avoid completely.

- styrofoam
- disposable nappies
- aerosols: deodorant, hair spray, room freshener, spray starch
- nonrechargeable batteries
- milk and fruit juices in cartons (which are made from bleached paper and have been found to contain dioxins)
- toilet paper made from paper which has been bleached
- plastic cutlery and other disposable products
- mercury thermometers
- over-packaged goods.

Section 5

THE GARDEN OF EDEN

At the beginning of this book we spoke of the Garden of Eden and its significance for us today. We do not repeat that discussion here. We add, simply, that the Creator must delight in plants and animals. Picture God walking through the garden, tending plants, petting animals and showing Adam and Eve the special care he gives to a delicate morning bloom or night-crawler. It's more natural for us to care for the garden than we probably know.

We care for the garden for another reason as well: it is linked to our survival. Destruction of God's creation is, in the long run, destruction of what sustains our life. In that sense, environmental concern is the ultimate pro-life issue. We suggest five ways to work the garden.

36

Save a Tree

Trees are intimately linked to our survival. One of the most basic lessons regarding nature—we learn it in primary school—is that we exhale carbon dioxide, while trees inhale it. They in turn exhale oxygen and we inhale it. Our ability to breathe is interlocked with their ability to breathe.

If you have wondered why there is all the fuss over the destruction of the Amazon rainforests, well, this is one of the main reasons. The Amazon basin holds the world's largest collection of trees and essentially is the earth's lungs. Our planet will not survive without its lungs.

The forests also help protect the planet from extreme heat. The earth is warmed by the sun's energy. Some of this heat escapes into space, but some is trapped by 'greenhouse gases' in the upper atmosphere—the 'greenhouse effect'. When the trees are destroyed, carbon dioxide—the main greenhouse gas—cannot be taken up naturally. Too much carbon dioxide in the atmosphere increases the greenhouse effect and leads to a rise in global temperatures.

Another way our forests protect the earth is by preventing soil erosion. Millions of tonnes of good topsoil run off into the oceans every year, stripping the land of its best growing soil. Several countries in the world today experience famine precisely for this reason.

A final means by which the trees are linked to our survival is rain. Believe it or not, the drought that has regularly ravaged Ethiopia and Sudan over the last decade was caused primarily by the deforestation of the Amazon basin. These gargantuan lungs put moisture back into the air through a process called transpiration, forming rain clouds that are then blown over the ocean by winds and finally 'bust loose' in the region of Ethiopia and Sudan. Removing the Amazon's trees removes Africa's rain supply.

The World Wide Fund for Nature (WWF) is one organisation working to save forests around the world. In order to conserve forests, WWF believes protected areas must be established and is campaigning to ensure that at least 10 per cent of tropical rainforests are afforded some degree of official protection by the year 2000. WWF also believes that the use of natural resources such as timber should be sustainable, and that forests should be properly managed to guarantee their long-term survival.

We can all help to save trees and releaf the planet.

- Plant a tree in your garden (consult your local nursery or garden centre for the best species, method, and position). Consider doing this once each year if you have the space.
- Talk to local officials about retaining a certain number of trees in new development projects. Cement suburbs suffer from a quiet deforestation.
- Encourage your council to get trees back to the parks and pavements.
- Donate funds to the World Wide Fund for Nature every time you donate funds to a hunger relief organisation.
- Use fewer paper products.
- Avoid products made from tropical hardwoods.

37

Releaf at Christmas

Christmas rolls around once every year, and part of the traditional ritual is to go out and buy a cut tree, put on some Christmas music, eat mince pies and decorate the tree.

We don't want to meddle with a tradition, we just want to suggest an adjustment.

Buy a *live* Christmas tree. You will have to pay more for it initially, but in the long run you will have helped save the planet.

Be sure to plan ahead so that you're not caught off guard ten days before Christmas. Sometime in November, talk to your friendly nursery or garden centre manager. Find out what size tree is most reasonable to cart to your home (root ball and all), and ask to have one reserved for you.

Work out in advance what you will do with the tree. Locate (with advice) a spot in your garden where it can thrive and add beauty. If you keep your house cool enough, the tree may survive well in the usual spot inside, covered with ornaments, till Christmas is over and you plant it out-doors. If not, begin a new tradition of planting your Christmas tree when it arrives and decorating it outdoors with weatherproof lights and ornaments.

If your property is large enough, you will be able to create quite a park to mark your care of the environment.

If you live in a flat and have no garden, well before

Christmas you can contact a land-owning friend or an institution with large grounds that would be interested in taking your live tree after the holidays.

38

A Bird in the . . .

Trees attract birds. The birds 'stake out' their territory and
build their homes, and their constant singing entertains us
while reminding us of the biblical teaching that even if
humans stop praising God, the rest of creation certainly will
not.

We suggest that you bring birds into your life if they
currently are not there. Two good methods are easy for any
of us to work on, possibly with the help of a friend or two. If
you have children, let them contribute their creativity to the
effort.

Make a home

Build a nesting-box. These can range from a simple basic
design to an elaborate thatched cottage style. Pick a model
that fits your skill. Your library should carry books giving
you instructions. Check them out, and as a family choose
your model, purchase the materials and then build the
nesting-box as a group effort. Research the type of birdseed
you need to attract these little flying wonders, so that when
your project is complete you will be ready. If possible, have
the nesting-box within view of a large window—this way you
can enjoy watching the residents from indoors. Once the
baby birds are hatched, the parents will be darting in and out
to feed the ever-open beaks. But make sure the nesting-box

is sheltered from the midday-sun—if the babies get too hot
they will die—and protected from cats and squirrels.

Feeding time

Another simple project is to build a birdtable. Birds love to
swoop down and feed, especially during the winter months.
Again, check out a book or design your own table. Once
your project is complete, put out some meat trimmings, fat,
bread or birdseed to attract the first round of diners. Once
the word is out you'll have no problem getting more clients.

With a minimum of upkeep required, you've added a
family hobby and a set of memories, given yourselves a
chance to observe some of God's wonderful creatures up
close and (where winter is severe) helped the birds stay alive
as food gets scarce.

39

Green Thumb It

A little gardening can go a long way towards helping us stay close to the miracle of life. The seed dies and is buried, and then it is raised to bloom and bear fruit.

This continual cycle of the earth's giving birth repeats the wonder of creation billions of times over, throughout the world, every day of spring. We recommend that you experiment a little with the life of the earth. Pick a project that suits your lifestyle and limits, because the goal is to enjoy the process and learn. If a certain project seems too big and overwhelming, stay away from it. If you live in a flat, begin with something as simple as a window-box.

Don't go it alone. Always remember that friendly garden centre manager who wants your business. Explain your goals and you will get all the free advice you need.

Go organic

As much as possible, experiment with natural care of the earth instead of using chemicals. To get started, listen to the advice given on TV and radio gardening programmes. Or borrow some books on organic gardening from the library. The principle here is to make the soil healthy without introducing toxins that initially give plants a boost but in the long term poison the soil and water system. Pesticides and weed killers are the particular criminals in this regard. Most garden centres can provide you with natural pesticides or put you in touch with a mail-order company that provides them.

Here's your chance to experiment with composting too. If you have a garden, begin a little compost heap with your grass clippings, vegetable peelings, fruit rinds and cores, and any other organic matter and watch your garden grow. Most gardening books give simple guidance on how to get your compost heap going and maintained. It doesn't smell bad; it helps save the planet.

40

Don't Be a Dodo

As many as 1,000 species are being eliminated from the earth every day. This figure is really beyond our comprehension, but it clearly illustrates to us that the garden is losing inhabitants that can never be replaced.

Unfortunately, the discussion of endangered species has too often been carried out by political extremists who do not talk with each other—they only shout their opinions in the other party's face and by their behaviour perpetuate the problem.

Our recommendation is this: don't be a dodo. Take an interest in the creation and learn from people of differing views. Often the issues related to endangered species are connected to people's livelihood. Consequently, the stakes are high, and the issue appears to be narrowed down to an either/or proposition: the creature's life or mine. In this country, for instance, some insects will become extinct because to save them would require large changes in land management.

It's important to take an interest in endangered species, because each of them reflects a unique touch of God's creative hand. We should not avoid the subject just because it is surrounded by controversy. Some of the best approaches, we feel, involve simple education. Decide to read one book on endangered species this year. Ask your librarian for guidance. Don't begin with something technical. Next, take an interest in your geographic region. Why not join your local Wildlife Trust? The Royal Society for Nature Conservation Wildlife Trusts Partnership is made up of forty-seven local Wildlife Trusts and fifty urban Wildlife Groups. Find out what special creation of God (be it plant or animal) indigenous to your area is threatened—and whether there's anything you can do to help save it. Learn and celebrate God's artistry.

You may eventually find yourself drawn into regional issues that seem to pit human well-being against the rest of creation. We encourage you to participate as much as your learning allows, and we urge that your respect for God's creation be matched by your respect of God's character. That is, always conduct yourself in a godly manner that is gentle and humble and that shows high regard for your brothers and sisters, for they are your equals whether or not they agree with your views.

Section 6

ADVOCATE

Some of you have the special skills and gifts that go with taking a public stand, calling companies and governments to account for their abuses and pointing to a new or alternative way. Some of you hold positions of influence so that a very small decision on your part can positively affect many people and a large portion of the environment. In this section of the book we are calling for leadership.

We want to stress that all leadership is to be conducted in the spirit of compassion, servanthood, teachability and camaraderie. Stories of environmental advocates who destroy property and endanger the lives of other human beings in order to make their point chill us. That behaviour does not reflect a true compassion for creation (humans are the crown of God's creation), nor does it reflect a personal encounter with the personal Creator.

We hope that many of our readers will take leadership to stand in the gap, and we offer five ways you can make a difference.

41

Celebrate!

People who are involved in environmental concerns and issues of social justice are often caricatured as being in a bad mood. And that's more accurate than not—unfortunately, the encounter with abuse robs the activist of joy. Yet the *celebration* of God's good creation and character is the real basis for environmental activism.

The United Nations celebrate World Environment Day on 5th June. We suggest you make it an annual celebration. Here are a few possibilities:

- If you are a member of a church or fellowship, arrange well in advance for the Sunday sermon and all Sunday school lessons, on the Sunday nearest World Environment Day, to be centred on the creation and God's call to us to tend the garden.
- Work with the local school to sponsor an arts and crafts display by students reflecting their interest in and understanding of environmental concerns. Ask the local library to display these pieces during that week.
- Put together an all-day concert of local talent on the Saturday nearest the day. Sponsor a plant-a-tree drive to go with the celebration, and put on a party with some good food. (*Clean up* the area after the celebration is over.)
- See if your town is willing to decorate the high street during the two weeks that surround World Environment

Day, in the same way it decorates for Christmas. This could become an annual event, and the local schools could plan a parade.

42

Educate

People often fail to get involved in caring for the environment simply because it all seems too big to grasp. And some feel that our destruction has already gone too far, 'so why rearrange the deckchairs on the *Titanic*?'

This is where your leadership comes in. Get a feel for the people around you. Try to understand the level at which they have grasped environmental concerns and the aspirations that motivate or fears that block their involvement. Set up educational opportunities accordingly. We recommend the following as possible means towards education:

- Sponsor with your local library a half-day seminar on the environment.
- Work with your local schools. See if they will let you do a one-hour presentation in each of their classrooms (this could be a year-long commitment).
- Approach local churches. Offer your services to do a presentation for them in one of their regular slots—for example, Friday youth group, Wednesday prayer meeting or Sunday school.
- Get the local pastors together and see if they would be interested in a co-ordinated church effort that would sponsor an all-day seminar on the environment. You could offer to do all the legwork and co-ordinate the presentations. The cost per participant should be kept to a minimum just to cover the materials—say £1.50 per

person, adding £2.50 if the person wants lunch. Be sure to have several resources on hand for sale, and if the season is right, see if your local garden centre would put certain trees and flowers on display, both for educational purposes and for sale.

43

Write the Wrong

We mentioned earlier in this book that companies are very sensitive to the consumer. When the green movement made a few flash appearances during the past decade, the business response was 'Wait and see.' That has changed to the point where businesses now *fear* the anti-green label. We suggest a few ways you can influence companies.

Begin on home territory

If you work for a local business, take a couple of lunch hours to do an inventory of the stockroom. Make a list of all the materials bought from companies unfriendly to the environment. The evidence will be clear enough: Are the products made from recycled or recyclable materials? If not, research alternative suppliers that can deliver the goods at the same cost, and then approach your supervisors with the data. When changing over to the new suppliers, contact the former suppliers with your reasons. Explain that you will go back to them when they reform their ways.

Go for the big hitters

In the States, McDonald's could not run and hide. Determined to break down that fast-food chain's intransigence regarding styrofoam, an American environmental organisation forced it to agree, in a defensive posture, to abandon styrofoam. The pen was used by advocates in two ways.

The McDonald's headquarters was deluged by letters proclaiming a boycott of the chain until behaviour changed. That was private but strong enough to get attention.

The same activists began writing letters to the editors of local and national publications, drawing attention to the abuses by McDonald's. Editors picked up on the idea and published strong, well-researched pieces that showed the negative impact McDonald's had on the environment. McDonald's had to change or lose business. It chose to change.

You can do the same in this country where, because no pressure has been brought to bear, McDonald's still use styrofoam instead of paper packaging. Or link up with a couple of friends and make a project out of a supermarket run. Pick three or four products that show absolutely no (or very little) regard for the environment, and then spend an evening together writing letters of protest or concern to the manufacturers. In your letter, list companies that offer the same product or service in an environmentally sound manner. Those to whom you write need to know that an alternative idea works *and* that consumers can make the choice to switch to another available supplier. Write to your local newspaper editor, too, and if you have skills in journalism, do a few freelance pieces on your discoveries.

Send a good word

Companies that have made the effort to change need to know that you appreciate their sensitivity. Use all the ideas from the previous suggestions, but in a *positive* form. Thank these companies for being environmentally responsible and let them know that they have your business. Caring for the environment requires true partnership, and companies are willing to make necessary changes if they are sure that consumers will put their money where their mouth is.

44

Mark Your 'X'

Voting is the heartbeat of democracy. Our entire system is based on the notion that government has no function outside the will of the people. Citizens who choose not to influence government through their votes are either very content with the way things are (and don't sense a change around the corner) or do not believe that their vote makes a difference. We are suggesting that both of these positions are hazardous to the environment.

Influence the government with your knowledge of the issues and your concern. (To save time, work with several friends, each of you reading certain reports and publications and then sharing what you've learned.) There are several levels for involvement, including the following:

- Let local councillors know that you are watching their performance in the light of forthcoming elections. Let them know your *specific* concerns.
- Do the same with your local MP. He or she is vulnerable to your influence. Let him know if you approve or disapprove of his environmental performance, and tell him in specific terms what changes you seek.
- In the run-up to a local (or general) election, write letters to the editor of a local (national) newspaper to address the track record of specific candidates.
- Publish leaflets or guides for election week, showing

where the different candidates stand on caring for the planet.

- Finally, let the Prime Minister know what you think about his performance.

The resource section of this book has the appropriate addresses for your MP, MEP and the Prime Minister.

45

Make a Scene

Some personality types function well in public confrontation. We need these people, because too many environmental injustices are perpetuated for no other reason than the absence of voices that will clearly and publicly condemn the abuses.

If you live near an environmental abuser and have the personality for protest, seek a meeting with the offending company. Make sure you have done your research well so that your presentation is truthfully convincing and helpful. Be gracious but firm. Make it clear that if change does not occur, you will attempt to launch a public protest against the firm. If change is not forthcoming, contact Friends of the Earth or Greenpeace for advice (you may be able to obtain names and addresses of supporters in your region), and go for it.

Your local churches may also want to lend their voice to the protest. Nothing is as spiritually invigorating and forceful as an all-night candlelight prayer vigil at the gates of an environmental culprit. You may discover the media's support of this approach. Christian groups, unfortunately, are not known for these sensitivities, so it is newsworthy when Christians do show their public commitment to environmental care.

Perhaps you have the funds to influence certain companies' environmental practices. If so, link up with a few friends to buy shares in an abusive company. Show up at the annual general meeting and voice your legitimate concerns as a part owner of the company. Again, be sure you have done first-class research, and work to present an excellent description of the issues and alternatives involved. Remember, your goal is not to be seen, it's to implement change. You may even discover a very friendly board of directors who will call you into their offices for a more complete presentation of the issues.

Section 7

RESOURCES FOR ACTION

What you have in these final pages is a fairly thorough resource list for activists who want to get a basic library together and who want to know where to go and whom to contact to make the environmental voice heard.

We are convinced that every small step makes a big difference, so we hope that this resource section encourages you to implement even further the ideas in this book which have caught your fancy. We offer five categories of resources.

46

Magazines

Here are some publications which will help you do your part to save the planet.

BBC Wildlife Magazine

A monthly magazine with popular but scientifically accurate articles on wildlife and conservation, both national and international. Some are linked by subject to TV and radio programmes. £1.75 per month.

Earth Matters

Friends of the Earth's flagship magazine, published quarterly and circulated to all members. Each issue contains updates on campaigns and indepth features on particular issues. Contact Friends of the Earth, 26–28 Underwood Street, London N1 7JQ. Telephone: 071-490 1555.

The Ecologist

This is for the serious reader. The magazine contains fully referenced articles on economic, social and environmental affairs written from an ecological standpoint. £3.00 per year (six issues).

Green Magazine

This monthly magazine includes topical news and feature articles on all aspects of the environment. £1.95 per month.

Natural World

The magazine of the Royal Society for Nature Conservation, issued to all members. Contains updates and short articles on nature conservation. Contact RSNC, The Green, Witham Park, Waterside South, Lincoln LN5 7JR. Telephone: 0522 544400.

47

Books

Look for these titles in your local bookshop or library. If you can't find the ones you want, ask the shop or library to order them for you.

Button, John. *New Green Pages*. Macdonald Optima: London, 1990.
Christensen, Karen. *Home Ecology*. Arlington Books: London, 1989.
Elkington, John and Hailes, Julia. *The Green Consumer Guide*. Gollancz: London, 1988.
Elkington, John. *Young Green Consumer Guide*. Gollancz: London, 1990.
Porritt, Jonathon (ed). *Friends of the Earth Handbook*. Macdonald Optima: London, 1990.
Seymour, John and Giradet, Herbert. *Blueprint for a Green Planet*. Dorling Kindersley: London, 1988.
Wells, Phil and Jetter, Mandy. *The Global Consumer*. Gollancz: London, 1990.

48

Government Departments

Here are some addresses to use when requesting information or registering concern.

Department of Energy
1 Palace Street
London SW1E 5HE
071-238 3370

Department of the Environment
2 Marsham Street
London SW1P 3EB
071-276 3000

Department of Health
Richmond House
79 Whitehall
London SW1
071-210 3000

Department of Trade and Industry
Environment Unit
151 Buckingham Palace Road
London SW1W 9SS
071-215 5000

Ministry of Agriculture, Fisheries and Food
Whitehall Place
London SW1
071-270 8080

Write to your MP at

House of Commons
Westminster
London SW1A 0AA

To find the name of your MP phone the House of Commons Information Office on
071-219 4272

Write to your MEP at

Centre Européen
Kirchberg
Luxembourg

To find the name and UK address of your MEP phone the European Parliament Information Office on
071-222 0411

Write to the Prime Minister at

10 Downing Street
London SW1A 2AA

49

Recycling: Information and Associations

Alcan Aluminium Can Recycling
Eldon House
Regent Centre
Gosforth
Newcastle-upon-Tyne
NE3 3PW
0670 813811

Aluminium Can Recycling
Association
I-Mex House
52 Blucher Street
Birmingham B1 1QU
021-633 4656

Aluminium Foil Recycling
Campaign
38–42 High Street
Bidford-on-Avon
Worcs M50 4AA
0789 490609

Association of British Reclaimed
Rubber Manufacturers
First Avenue
Trafford Park
Manchester M17 1DT
061-872 1424

Association of Recycled Paper
Suppliers
Bow Triangle Business Centre
Unit 2
Eleanor Street
London E3 4NP
081-980 2233

British Carton Association
11 Bedford Row
London WC1R 4DX
071-242 686201

British Glass Manufacturers
Federation
Northumberland Road
Sheffield S10 2UA
0742 686201

British Paper & Board Industry
Federation Ltd
Papermakers House
Rivenhall Road
Swindon SN5 7BE
0793 886086

British Plastics Federation
5 Belgrave Square
London SW1X 8PO
071-235 9483

British Scrap Federation
(ferrous metals)
16 High Street
Brampton
Huntingdon
Cambs PE1 8TU
0480 455249

British Secondary Metals
Association
(non-ferrous metals)
25 Park Road
Runcorn
Cheshire WA7 4SS
09285 72400

British Waste Paper Association
Alexander House Business
Centre
Station Road
Aldershot
Hants GU11 1BQ
0252 344454

Can Makers Information Service
36 Grosvenor Gardens
London SW1W 0EB
071-629 9621

Chemical Recovery Association
(solvents and waste oil)
9 Larch Grove
Paddock Wood
Tonbridge
Kent TN12 6LA
0892 833587

Community Recycling Network
140 Devonshire Street
Sheffield
0742 759886

Federation of Resource Centres
(scrapstores)
c/o Playworks
25 Bullivant Street St Ann's
Nottingham
0602 582659

Independent Waste Paper
Processors Association
25 High Street
Daventry
Northants NN11 4BG
03272 703223

INCPEN
(Industry Council for Packaging
and the Environment)
Premier House
10 Greycoat Place
London SW1P 1SB
071-222 8866

National Association of Waste
Disposal Contractors
Mountbarrow House
6/20 Elizabeth Street
London SW1W 9RB
071-824 8882

National Tyre Recycling
Association
The Meadows
Ryleys Lane
Alderley Edge
Cheshire SK9
0625 582346

Oxfam Wastesaver
Unit 4–6
Ringway Industrial Estate
Beck Road
Huddersfield HG1 5DG
0484 542021

Plastics Recycling Ltd
Sales Office
60 Blackpole Trading Estate
Worcester WR3 9SQ
0905 55410

Reclamation Association
(textiles)
16 High Street
Brampton
Huntingdon
Cambs PE18 8TU
0480 455249

RECOUP (Recycling of Used
Plastic Containers)
Manor Barn
Polebrook
Nr Oundle
Peterborough
Cambs PE8 5LN
0832 274759

Save-a-Can
Elm Lane
19 Elmshott Lane
Chippenham
Slough
Berks SL1 5QS
0628 666658

Save Waste and Prosper
(SWAP)
(consultancy and training)
PO Box 19
6–8 Great George
Leeds LS1 6TF
0532 438777

Steel Can Recycling Information
Bureau
Kingsgate House
536 Kings Road
London SW10 0TE
071-351 5208

United Kingdom Reclamation
Council
16 High Street
Brampton
Huntingdon
Cambs PE18 8TU
0480 455249

Warren Spring Laboratory
Recycling Advisory Unit
Gunnels Wood Road
Stevenage
Herts SG1 2BX
0438 741122

Waste Watch
c/o NCVO
26 Bedford Square
London WC1B 3HU
071-636 4066

50

National Organisations

Each of these organisations is concerned for the environment. Write or phone to inquire about their activities and resource materials.

British Trust for Conservation
Volunteers
36 St Mary's Street
Wallingford
Oxon OX10 0EU
0491 39766

Centre for Alternative
Technology
Education Office
Llywngwern Quarry
Machynlleth
Powys
Wales
0654 703743

Friends of the Earth
26–28 Underwood Street
London N1 7JQ
071-490 1555

Greenpeace
30–31 Islington Green
London N1 8XE
071-354 5100

Henry Doubleday Research
Association
National Centre for Organic
Gardening
Ryton-on-Dunsmore
Coventry CV8 3LG
0203 303517

National Society for
Clean Air
136 North Street
Brighton
Sussex BN1 1RG
0273 26313

Nature Conservancy
Council
Northminster House
Northminster Road
Peterborough
Cambs PE1 1UA
0733 40345

Royal Society for Nature
Conservation
The Green
Witham Park
Waterside South
Lincoln LN5 7JR
0522 544400

Royal Society for the Prevention
of Cruelty to Animals
The Causeway
Horsham
West Sussex RH12 1HG
0403 264181

Royal Society for the Protection
of Birds
The Lodge
Sandy
Bedfordshire SG19 2DL
0767 80551

Tidy Britain Group
The Pier
Wigan WN3 4EX
0942 824620

World Wide Fund For Nature
Panda House
Weyside Park
Catteshall Lane
Godalming
Surrey GU7 1XR
0483 426444

50 Ways You Can Feed A Hungry World

by Tony Campolo & Gordon Aeschliman

You already want to help hungry people, at home and overseas. Your only question: 'How?' This practical manual is just what you need. Here are fifty options to choose from. Ideas like:

- diverting personal funds quickly and fairly painlessly
- donating your professional skills
- joining an organisation that helps get food to hungry areas
- going on a weekend break in a needy area
- considering a career that directly impacts the world food situation.

Some of the ideas in this book will take you thirty minutes; some will take thirty weeks. Some will cost a postage stamp; some will require an investment of thousands of pounds. Some are for an individual or family to do; some will take a whole church or community group.

Ready to do something? Here are fifty good places to start.

TONY CAMPOLO is Professor of Sociology at Eastern College in St Davids, Pennsylvania, the author of many bestselling books, and a popular speaker at conferences including Spring Harvest and Greenbelt.

GORDON AESCHLIMAN has been concerned for the massive needs around us in an unjust and hungry world ever since his childhood in South Africa. Formerly editor of *World Christian*, he is currently a freelance writer and speaker.

 Kingsway Publications